D1278105

The Little People's
Bible

Illustrated by Maria Pascual

ST. PAUL BOOKS & MEDIA

ISBN 0-8198-4477-2

Original title: *La Biblia de Los Ninos*
by Eugenio Sotillos
© 1988, Oceáno Grupo Editorial, S.A., Barcelona

French edition: Nathalie Brock

Translated from the French by Marianne Trouvé, FSP
Adapted by Eileen Heffernan, FSP

English edition copyright © 1995, Daughters of St. Paul

Produced by Slovart Print s.r.o., Bratislava, Slovakia

Published by Pauline Books & Media, 50 St. Paul's Avenue, Boston, MA 02130.
Pauline Books & Media is the publishing house of the Daughters of St. Paul, an international congregation of women religious serving the Church with the communications media.

1 2 3 4 5   99 98 97 96 95

CONTENTS

Part One
The Old Testament

Part Two
The New Testament

Part One
The Old Testament

The Creation of the World

This story begins a very, very long time ago. There wasn't any world yet—no sky, no land, no water. But God was already there.

God was alone. Then he decided to make our world. When God makes something, that is called "creating." This was a big job and God took six days to create everything.

On the first day, God created light and darkness—the day and the night.

The second day, he created the sky and the land. On the third day, God separated the water from the earth. He called the dry part the "land," and the water, the "sea." The earth was still bare. So then God covered the earth with

grass, plants and fruit trees. On the fourth day, God thought,

"I'm going to create the sun to light up the day, and the moon for the night." On the fifth day, God said to himself, "The earth needs some animals!" So God put the fish in the sea, and the birds in the sky. He told them, "Have many little fish and little birds."

Then, God saw that everything was good, and he created other kinds of animals. On the sixth day, he said, "Now, I'm going to create people. They will be a little bit like me. They will take care of the world." On the seventh day, God rested.

Adam and Eve

God created the first man and called him Adam. God gave him a very beautiful garden called Eden. But God saw that Adam was bored all by himself. So God said, "He needs a friend." He made Adam fall asleep. Then he took a rib from Adam's side and created a woman, whom he called Eve. Then God gave an order to the two of them, "You can eat all the fruits in the garden, except the fruit from the forbidden tree. If you eat it, you'll die."

For a while, Adam and Eve lived very happily. But the

devil was hiding nearby, watching them. One day, to trick them, the devil took the form of a snake and whispered to Eve, "If you eat that forbidden fruit, you won't really die. You'll become like God."

Eve disobeyed God and ate the fruit which the devil offered her. She got Adam to eat it, too. Then they felt ashamed and ran to hide. Suddenly, God appeared. Adam tried to make excuses by saying, "It's Eve's fault."

Eve made an excuse, too. She said, "It's the snake's fault!"

Then God cursed the devil and sent Adam and Eve out of Eden. He said, "From now on, you'll have to work hard for your living. Things won't be given to you for free!"

Cain and Abel

After they had been sent out of the garden, Adam and Eve cried for a long time. Later, they had two sons, Cain and Abel. When the boys grew up, Cain, the oldest, became a farmer. Abel tended sheep. The two brothers offered some gifts to God. Cain burned the fruits of his harvest on an altar, while Abel killed and burned the finest sheep from his flock. But one day Cain grumbled, "It's strange that God seems to like Abel's gifts better than mine."

Cain got jealous and grew angry at Abel. So one day, God

14

asked Cain, "Why are you so angry and jealous? If you do something good, you will be happy. But if you do something bad, you'll commit sin and then you'll be unhappy."

Cain didn't listen to God, but decided to kill Abel. One day he said to Abel, "Let's go out in the field." Once they got there, Cain killed Abel.

Then God asked Cain, "Where is your brother?"

"I don't know," Cain shot back. "Am I my brother's keeper?"

Very displeased, God told Cain, "Your brother's voice cries out to me for justice. From now on, you'll be an outcast. The land will no longer produce food for you, and you will wander over the earth."

"But anyone I meet might kill me," said Cain sadly.

"No," God answered. "If anyone kills you, that person will be punished even more. I'm going to put a mark on you that everyone will recognize. Now go far away from here!"

Noah's Ark

Seth was Adam and Eve's third son. He was a good man, and his children were called "children of God." They lived to be very old.

Noah belonged to Seth's family. One day out in the countryside, Noah heard God say, "People are doing very bad things. I'm going to send a

16

flood to destroy them, because I'm sorry that I created them."

But Noah was a good man. God told him what to do so that he and his family would be safe.

"Build an ark out of strong wood," God said. "Put your whole family on it, along with two animals of every kind." (An "ark" is a closed box.) God wanted Noah to build a boat that was all closed up.

When Noah's neighbors saw him building the ark, they made fun of him, "Why are you making a boat so far away from the sea?"

Noah warned them, "Because of our sins, God is going to punish us!" But no one listened to Noah. When the ark was ready, he and his family got on, along with all the animals. It was a calm day. But after Noah closed the door of the ark, rain began to pour down, and water flooded the whole earth.

The Flood

The rain poured down for forty days and forty nights. Everything drowned except Noah, his family, and all the animals in the ark. The ark floated calmly on the water. Finally, the rain stopped. The ark came to rest on a mountain and Noah sent out a black bird called a raven. The bird flew around and came back.

Noah said, "The earth hasn't dried out enough yet, because the raven has nowhere to perch."

A little later, Noah sent out a white bird called a dove. The second time he let it out, the dove came back carrying an olive branch in its beak. "This means that the land is now dry," Noah thought. Then they all left the ark and saw a rainbow.

God spoke and told them, "Go live on the land, and have many children and grandchildren." Noah thanked God, because without God, Noah's family would have died like everyone else. God was pleased with Noah and told him, "I punished the people because they were doing very bad things. But now, all that is over. I won't send such a punishment again. Everything can start out fresh." Then God blessed Noah and his family. "I want you to be happy," he said.

The Tower of Babel

Some time later, Noah's sons Shem, Ham and Japheth left their father's house with their families. Ham and his family went to live between the Tigris and the Euphrates Rivers. Japheth and his family traveled to Asia Minor and Greece. Shem took his family to the plains of Sumer, and they called themselves Semites.

One day, some people decided to build a very tall building called a tower. They wanted to show how great they were. "We'll build a tower up to heaven," they said. "We'll show that we are important—like God."

Everybody began to work on the tower. "It will be the tallest tower that anyone has ever built," they told each other.

But this didn't please God, who thought, "They think that if they build this tower, they'll be like me. But they're wrong.

Right now, they speak only one language. But from now on, they'll speak many different languages. Since they won't understand each other, they won't be able to work together."

How surprised the people were when they couldn't understand each other! They had to stop building the tower. We call it the "Tower of Babel," which mans "confusion," since the people couldn't understand each other. They all left and went in different directions.

Abraham and Sarah

Many years later, a man in Shem's family lived in a city called Ur. This man was named Abraham. Abraham loved God deeply. One day, God said to him, "Leave here, and go to the place that I will show you."

Abraham obeyed and left with his wife Sarah, who was very beautiful. His nephew Lot also went, and they brought their sheep and goats with them. They went to the land of Canaan. The trip took a long time. When they finally got there, God said, "This is the land that I've promised you, both you and your family. Your family will become a great nation."

But they could hardly find anything to eat, so Abraham decided to go to Egypt. The Egyptians treated Abraham well. His family grew, and he became even richer than before. Lot also did well. Later, Abraham and Sarah and Lot went back to the land God had promised to Abraham.

But then Abraham's shepherds and Lot's shepherds began to argue about who would get the best part of the land. So Abraham told Lot, "You take the better part of the land, and I'll take another." Lot agreed and they went in different directions.

The Sacrifice of Isaac

Time went by. Now Abraham was very old. Sarah was very old, too, but one day she had a baby boy. They named him Isaac. The little family lived a happy life together for a few years. But one day, God decided to see if Abraham loved God more than anything else. He called out, "Abraham!"

"Here I am, Lord," Abraham answered.

"Now, pay attention, because this is what I'd like you to do," said God. "Take your only son Isaac, whom you love so much. Go to the land of Moriah, and offer Isaac to me as a sacrifice on a mountain that I will show you." This was like what Abel did with his sheep. But Isaac was a *boy.*

Abraham obeyed and left with Isaac. Abraham was crying. Near the mountain, Isaac asked, "Father, we have the wood, but where is the gift to offer to God?"

"God will give us one, my son," Abraham replied. When they climbed to the top of the mountain, Abraham built an altar. He piled up the wood, then tied Isaac to it. But when he was ready to kill Isaac, an angel came and said, "Stop! Don't hurt the boy, because God is pleased with your obedience."

Abraham was very happy. He saw a ram caught by its horns in a nearby bush. Abraham took it and offered it to God instead of Isaac. The angel promised Abraham, "Because you have obeyed, God will give you happiness, and someday your family will be very big."

Jacob's Dream

Isaac grew up and married a girl named Rebecca. They had two sons, Esau and Jacob. Once, Jacob went on a long trip. He had to walk. One night, he stopped near a hill and found a place to sleep. He had a strange dream. He saw a ladder that went all the way up to the stars. There were angels going up and down on it. Then God said to Jacob:

"I am the God of Abraham and Isaac. This land on which you are resting is for you. I am going to make your land bigger, and I'll do good things for your whole family." When Jacob woke up, he thought about his dream and said to himself, "God is here in this

place, and I didn't know it."

He took the rock he had used for a pillow and stood it on end. It would mark the spot where God had spoken to him. He poured oil on it to thank God. Then he said, "I will call this place 'Bethel,' which means 'the house of God.'"

Some time later, Jacob married a girl named Rachel. Jacob and Rachel had many children. One day, God repeated his promise. He said to Jacob, "I will no longer call you Jacob but Israel. Some day there will be many kings in your family."

Joseph and His Brothers

Jacob had twelve sons, but he was especially kind to Joseph. Joseph's brothers were jealous of him and hated him. One day, Joseph had a dream and told his brothers about it. "We were in the middle of a field, tying wheat into bunches. Suddenly, my bundle of wheat stood up straight, and your bundles bowed down in front of it."

His brothers were angry and told him, "So what are you trying to say? That you're going to be king over us?"

"I don't know," answered Joseph.

After this, Joseph had another dream which he told to his brothers. "I saw the sun, the moon and eleven stars bowing down before me." This made his brothers even more jealous.

One day, Jacob told Joseph, "Go and see if everything is all right with your brothers, who are watching the sheep."

"Look!" his brothers said when they saw Joseph coming. "Let's get rid of him. We can tell our father that a wild animal killed Joseph."

So they rushed up to Joseph, took his long shirt and sold him to some people who were passing by. Then they tore the shirt and put some goat blood on it. When they showed it to their father, he burst into tears. He thought Joseph was dead.

Joseph in Egypt

In Egypt Joseph was sold to be a slave. He was bought by Potiphar, who worked for the pharaoh, or king. Joseph became Potiphar's friend, because Joseph was honest and did good work. One day, Potiphar told him, "Because I like you, Joseph, I want you to look after my house and the other slaves."

"I'll be happy to do that," Joseph said.

So Joseph began to take care of the whole house. God did good things for him. But

Potiphar was married, and his wife, who was young and beautiful, began to fall in love with Joseph. She wanted Joseph to love her. But Joseph didn't want to. "No!" he told her. "It isn't right. I don't want to do anything bad to Potiphar."

"But we wouldn't tell anyone," she said.

"No!" Joseph repeated angrily.

One day, in a rage, Potiphar's wife tried to get hold of Joseph again. But he ran outside, leaving his cloak behind. The woman brought the cloak to her husband.

"Joseph can't be trusted," she told Potiphar. "He tried to hug me, but I screamed and he ran away."

Potiphar was angry. He had Joseph put in prison.

Pharaoh's Dreams

Joseph felt sad. He did not deserve to be in prison. To help him feel better, God sent him some people to talk to. One of them was an old servant of pharaoh, who promised he would try to get Joseph out of jail.

Meanwhile, in the royal palace, pharaoh had a dream that he was on the edge of a river. Suddenly, he saw seven ugly and thin cows come out of the river. They ate seven other beautiful, fat cows.

Then pharaoh had a second dream. This time he saw seven ears of grain, which were fat and healthy. Then seven thin ears ate the seven healthy ones. When pharaoh woke up, he felt disturbed about the dream. He called all the smartest men he knew and told them, "I'll give you a great reward if you can

explain my dreams."

For a long time the wise men tried to figure out the dreams, but they couldn't explain them. Suddenly, the old servant remembered Joseph and told pharaoh, "I know someone who can help you."

"Go and find him," pharaoh replied. Joseph came into the palace and listened to pharaoh. Then Joseph said, "For seven years, there will be rich harvests. But after that, people will die of hunger."

"I believe you," pharaoh told him. "But please help us!"

"Put a wise man in charge of storing up food," Joseph answered. "Then there will be food all the time."

"I'll count on you to be that man," pharaoh said. Then he gave Joseph a gold chain to thank him.

Joseph Meets His Brothers Again

Now Joseph wasn't a slave anymore. He was an important person in Egypt. At the end of the seven years of good harvests, bad weather came. There was no more grain in the fields. Then the people asked pharaoh for bread. He told them, "Don't worry! Go to Joseph. He'll give you some-thing to eat." And Joseph did.

In the land that Joseph came from, there wasn't any food either. So Joseph's father, Jacob, told Joseph's brothers to go to Egypt to buy grain. They went to see Joseph but did not recognize him. But Joseph recognized his brothers and told them, "You are enemies!"

"No!" his brothers said. "We have come from the land called Canaan. There are eleven of us brothers, counting Benjamin, the youngest, who stayed at home."

"Well then," answered Joseph, "I'm going to hold one of you as a prisoner until you return with your youngest brother. Then I'll believe you."

Later, when Benjamin came, Joseph hid a precious vase in his brother's bag. Then he said, "A thief! He's a thief!"

"Let him go," another brother pleaded. "Our father will die of sorrow if Benjamin doesn't come home. Punish me instead of him."

Joseph saw that his brothers had changed. He began to cry and told them who he was. They hugged each other.

35

Crossing the Desert

Back home, the brothers told their father the good news. "God has been so good to us," Jacob said. "My son is still alive! I want to see him before I die." So he started out with his whole family to meet Joseph again. They had to cross a desert.

One night, God appeared to Jacob. "Don't be afraid to

36

go to Egypt," God said. "There, I will make your family into a great nation."

"In a strange country?" asked Jacob.

"Yes," God replied. "I will be with you."

So Jacob continued along the way, with all his children and grandchildren. He told Judah, "My son, go and tell Joseph that we're here."

Full of joy, Joseph went to meet his father and brothers. He hugged them all very tightly. Jacob cried, "Now, I can die in peace, because I know that you are still alive."

As a gift, Joseph gave his father and his whole family the best fields in Egypt for their flocks of sheep and goats.

Baby Moses

Years passed by. Jacob died. Then Joseph died. But their family grew very large. There were hundreds of people in it, then thousands. They were called the Hebrews.

Some time later, there was a pharaoh who didn't like the Hebrew people. He said, "I don't want more Hebrews than Egyptians in my country."

So the pharaoh forced the Hebrews to be slaves. They had to work very hard. But they kept on having large families. Then the pharaoh ordered the soldiers, "Whenever a baby boy is born to the Hebrews, kill him by throwing him into the river."

One day, pharaoh's daughter went to swim in the river. She saw a basket floating on the water. When she opened it, she

was surprised to see a baby.
"Oh," she said, "it must be a
Hebrew baby. I will call him
Moses."

Slaves in Egypt

Pharaoh's daughter adopted Moses. He grew up, and people were kind to him, as if he was an Egyptian. But he often left the palace to try and help the other Hebrews, who were treated badly by the Egyptians. One day he saw a soldier beating up a Hebrew. He tried to defend the Hebrew, and without meaning to, he killed the soldier. He hid the body in the sand, hoping that no one would find it. But someone saw him. Moses was afraid of being arrested. He ran away to a land called Midian.

There, Moses learned how

to live in the desert. He became a shepherd. Years passed by. One day while Moses was watching the sheep, he saw a bush burning in a strange way. As he came closer, God spoke out of the fire.

"Moses! Moses!" said God, "I need you. I have seen that the Hebrews are suffering in Egypt. Set them free, and lead them here into the desert."

"But how can I bring them here with me? What if pharaoh doesn't want to let them go?" Moses asked.

"Don't be afraid!" God told him. "I will be with you."

The Plagues of Egypt

Moses went to pharaoh and asked pharaoh to let him lead all the Hebrews out of Egypt. "I don't know your God," pharaoh replied. "I'm not going to let them go."

Another time, Moses went back to pharaoh and asked again. "No way," pharaoh answered.

To show that he spoke for God, Moses threw a stick onto the ground and it turned into a snake. But this didn't make pharaoh change his mind. To scare pharaoh, Moses changed the color of all the water in Egypt. The water turned red, like blood. But pharaoh still didn't give in.

To help Moses, God sent other troubles to Egypt. They were called plagues. God sent thousands and thousands of

42

frogs, biting insects and flies which got into every house. A bad smell filled the whole country. Then the cows and sheep got sick. But pharaoh still said, "No."

Then God sent hail storms, which hurt the plants. After that, he told the Hebrews to mark their doors with blood

from a lamb. In each house of the Egyptians, which did not have this mark, somebody died. Finally, after this, pharaoh gave up and let Moses and the Hebrews leave Egypt.

The Crossing of the Sea

A great crowd of people left Egypt. Moses told them, "Always remember this day on which God set you free from being slaves."

Led by God, they crossed the desert as far as the Reed Sea. In order to show them the way, God appeared as a column of cloud by day, and a column of fire by night. But pharaoh was sorry that he had let them leave. He sent his army with horses and carts to chase the Hebrews.

When Moses got to the sea, he reached out his hand toward the water and a wonderful thing happened. The sea split in two, giving them a way to pass through it. All of the people walked through the sea on solid ground. The water stood like a wall on either side of them. But the Egyptian army was already right behind them and tried to pass between the walls of water. Moses held out the stick he carried, and the water closed behind the Hebrews. The sea went back where it had been before, and the Egyptian soldiers drowned.

The Hebrews were safe! They began to sing praises to God.

45

The Mysterious Manna

The Hebrews kept walking. But after long days of marching through the desert, they began to run out of food and water. "What are we going to eat? What are we going to drink?" they complained. "We were better off in Egypt!"

"God has not left us," Moses told them.

Right away, God sent them some birds like chickens for them to eat. But after more time on their long trip, they

again ran out of food and water. They became angry and complained against Moses. But the next morning when they woke up, they found that their camp was covered with small, white flakes.

"This is manna, the bread which God has sent you," Moses told them. "Gather it and then eat it."

The Hebrews ate the small flakes, which were sweet like honey. But after a while they had no more water. Obeying God, Moses hit a rock with his stick, and water came out. "Look how God has blessed us!" all the people cried out.

The Ten Commandments

Moses warned the people, "Don't complain anymore, because God is good and wants to help you." Moses was a great friend of God. God spoke to him often.

"Don't be afraid, Moses," God said. "I'll go ahead of you to lead you." When they came to Mount Sinai, God said, "Go up to the top of the mountain."

Moses obeyed. When he got to the top, God told him, "I am your God, and these are my commandments. You must not have other gods besides me. You must not say my name without respect. Keep the Lord's day holy. Be good to your father and your mother. You must not kill or steal, or say lies about anyone. You must not want to have your neighbor's wife. You must not want to take the things that other people have."

God gave Moses two flat pieces of stone on which these commandments were carved. Suddenly, the brightness of God showed itself before Moses. A great cloud and fire covered the top of the mountain. Moses stayed there praying for a long time. Then he came down from the mountain.

The Golden Calf

While Moses was on Mount Sinai, two other men took care of the camp. They were Aaron and Hur. But the time passed slowly. Moses was taking a long time to come back, and the people thought that he must have died. They quickly forgot about God, and began to make a golden statue of a calf to protect them. Everybody gave their gold and jewels in order to make the calf. When it was done, they began to pray to it. "This is our God

who brought us out of Egypt!" they cried.

When Moses came down from the mountain, he saw what the people were doing. He was angry. He threw down the stones with the commandments. They broke into many pieces. "Throw that statue into the fire!" Moses ordered.

The people did. Then they said they were sorry. Later, Moses went back up Mount Sinai and God gave him the commandments again. When Moses came down again, his face shone with a bright light. Then all the people shouted, "The Lord is our only God! We will always obey him."

51

The Ark of the Covenant

While Moses was up on the mountain, God said to him, "Tell the people to offer some of their gold, jewels and beautiful cloth to make things to use for prayer. In turn, I will always protect them. The priests must wear bright-colored clothes. Burn oil lamps which will smell like perfume.

"In order to pray together to me, you must make a very big tent for me. In it you will put the stones with the commandments."

Following God's orders, Moses built the tent. It had wooden walls that could be taken apart and carried. The roof was made of beautiful cloth. Inside, there were two parts, separated by a curtain. The first part had an altar and a candlestick with seven branches.

The second part contained a large box called the Ark of the Covenant. Inside it were

the stones with the commandments written on them. When everything was finished, a cloud came down from heaven. It showed that God was there. Led by the cloud, the Hebrews continued to walk through the desert to the promised land.

A New Leader

Some time after, God told Moses, "Take Joshua, who is a good man, and make him your helper. Tell the Hebrews to obey him."

Moses led Joshua to the priest Eleazar. All the Hebrew people were watching. Moses put his hands over Joshua and said that he would be the people's new leader. The people were happy and shouted, "Long live our new leader! We know that Joshua will be a good leader. He can lead our army into war against

our enemies, who are trying to stop us from going ahead."

"Joshua will lead us to victory!" they shouted with joy.

"With him, we will win!"

Then, following God's orders, Moses called the people together and told them, "We have to take one thousand men from each tribe (a group) for the army. We need at least twelve thousand soldiers to fight our enemies, who have tried to attack our camp several times."

So the army went out to fight, and they won a victory.

The Law of Moses

Moses again called the people together, and reminded them to obey the commandments. "This is what God says," Moses told them. "Listen to my voice! When you will cross the Jordan River and arrive in the land of Canaan, you must chase out all the people there. Then you will live in the land yourselves. This is the land that I have promised you."

The people answered, "Yes, Lord. We will do everything you have asked."

God then told Moses how

to divide the land. God also reminded Moses of what the people should do: love and serve God, show respect for other people, celebrate God's special days, help people in need, take care of animals, and not hurt birds that were raising families, besides many other things. At the end, God told him, "Don't be afraid of other nations, even though they may seem stronger than you. I will always help you."

The Promised Land

After many years in the desert, Moses and the people finally reached a place called Moab. There, God said to Moses, "Go up Mount Nebo." Moses obeyed and climbed to the top of the mountain. From there, he could see the land which God had promised them.

"This is the land which I promised to give to Abraham, Isaac and Jacob," God said. "You can look at it, but you yourself will not be able to enter it."

Moses looked at the land for a long time. After this, he died in the land of Moab, as God wanted. He was very old. The Hebrews spent thirty days

crying and remembering the good things Moses had done for them. Then God told Joshua, "Moses, my servant, is dead. Now you will take his place, and I will help you."

Joshua was a good leader, but Moses had been the best. He was buried in the land of Moab. No one knows where his grave is.

The Crossing of the Jordan

Joshua was now the only leader of the Hebrew people. They soon came to a river. On the other side was the promised land. But there was an enemy city on the other side, too. It was called Jericho. Joshua sent two men to see how the city was guarded. They came back and said, "We almost got caught, but a woman helped us hide." Then they added, "There are big walls around the city." "Oh," said someone else, "shouldn't we give up?"

"Don't say that!" Joshua answered. "Don't forget that God is with us and will help us."

"But how are we going to knock down the walls?" people asked.

"Don't worry," Joshua answered. "Those people are afraid of us. That's why they have walls."

60

After waiting three days, they crossed the Jordan River. As soon as the priests stepped into the water, it stopped flowing so they could pass through. When they got to the other side, Joshua said, "Go and get twelve stones from the river bed, one for each tribe, and set them up here. If someone later asks you what these stones are for, tell them, 'The people of Israel crossed the river here, just as they crossed the Reed Sea in past times.'"

61

The Conquest of Jericho

Strong walls stood all around the city of Jericho. No one could enter or leave the city. The people were afraid of Joshua and his soldiers. When Joshua got close to Jericho, he called the priests and told them, "March in front of the Ark of the Covenant, blowing your trumpets."

Then he told the rest of the people, "March around the city in silence and carry your weapons." Every day for seven days, they marched around Jericho. On the seventh day, the priests blew the trumpets and Joshua cried out, "Now shout out loud because God has given the city to us. We've

won the victory!"

Then they all shouted with a great cry and the walls of the city collapsed. Joshua and his soldiers ran into Jericho and fought to take it over. Then the Hebrews burned the city. All the gold and silver were put in the treasury of the Lord. After the city had been destroyed, Joshua warned the people, "God will punish anyone who tries to rebuild Jericho."

A Great New Leader

Some time later, Joshua too grew old and died. The Hebrews were sad and wondered, "What will happen now?"

For a while, they kept winning battles. The tribe (group) called Judah attacked many cities and towns. They always won. But then the Hebrews began to live like the people they had conquered. They started to pray to gods that weren't real. God was disturbed about this and no longer helped them in battle. So the Hebrews began to lose. After some years, they turned to God for help again. He told

64

the people, "You didn't listen to me, so I left you on your own. But now, listen to me! I have chosen Gideon to save you from your enemies."

To Gideon, God said, "You are very brave. I want you to destroy the altars of the false gods. Then build an altar to

pray to me."

Gideon obeyed God. Then with three hundred soldiers chosen by God, Gideon attacked the enemy camp. The enemies were frightened and ran away.

65

The Mighty Samson

For forty years, Gideon was a judge (leader) in Israel. But after he died, the Hebrews began to adore false gods again. So God left them on their own, and their enemies the Philistines made trouble for them.

One young Hebrew was chosen by God to help his people. His name was Samson, and he was very strong. Once, he killed a lion with only his bare hands. Another time Samson trapped three hundred foxes. He tied burning sticks called torches to their tails, then set them loose in the Philistines' fields. Everything burned down.

The Philistines were angry. They wanted to hurt Samson. So they caught him and tied him up. "Lord, help me!"

Samson cried out.

God helped him and made the ropes break. Samson picked up a big bone from the ground and attacked the Philistines. They were afraid and ran away.

"God is with me," Samson said, "because with this bone I have won against my enemies." After all that, he felt very thirsty and asked God, "Are you going to let me die of thirst?"

God made water flow out of a nearby rock. When Samson drank it, he felt strong again.

Samson and Delilah

Because Samson was so strong, the Philistines feared and hated him. They decided to kill him. One night, they saw Samson go into a house. They watched him, and closed all the gates of the city so he couldn't escape. When he woke up, Samson saw that his enemies had locked the gate. But he was so strong that he picked up the gate and got away.

Some time after, the Philistines found out that Samson loved a woman named Delilah. They went to see her and told her, "Try to find out why Samson is so strong. We'll pay you."

Later, Delilah asked Samson, "What makes you so strong?"

"I'm strong because my hair has never been cut,"

Samson answered. "I belong to God. If anyone cuts my hair, I'll become as weak as any other man."

Soon after, Delilah told this to the Philistines. Then, when Samson was asleep, she got a man to come and cut Samson's hair. When he woke up, the Philistines tied him with chains and made him blind. They made fun of him, saying, "Now where's your strength?"

Later, they chained Samson in a temple between two columns. "Lord," he cried out, "let me have my strength back! Let me get back at my enemies!" Then he shouted, "Now everyone will die!"

He pushed the columns apart. As they fell, the whole building collapsed and everyone in it died.

Samuel Chooses a King

Time passed, and the Philistines kept fighting against the Hebrews. So the Hebrews had a meeting and said, "Let's bring the Ark of the Covenant to our battles. Then God will help us."

But God left his people on their own. For a long time they had prayed to gods that weren't real. Since the Hebrews hadn't prayed to the real God, he didn't help them win more wars.

The Philistines captured the Ark of the Covenant. They put it in their own temple. But God punished the city which had the stolen Ark. So the Philistines were afraid and returned the Ark to the Hebrews.

There was a Hebrew named Samuel who would tell the people what God wanted. He was called a *prophet.*

The Hebrews told Samuel that they wanted a king to lead them in war. Samuel poured oil on the head of Saul to make him king. "You will lead God's people," Samuel said.

Thanks to Saul, the Hebrews won many victories.

Once, God ordered Saul to destroy the city of the Amalekites. Saul won the battle. But he disobeyed God because he kept the best things from the city. Seeing this, God was displeased and said, "I'm sorry that I chose Saul to be king. He disobeyed me. I will choose someone else to be king."

David and Goliath

King Saul began to feel sad. His servants wanted to cheer him up. So they suggested that he get a young boy named David to come and play the harp for him. Whenever David played his music,

King Saul felt much better.

A giant named Goliath lived in the land of the Philistines. One day, the giant came close to the Hebrew army and shouted, "Choose a man to come out and fight with me! If he kills me, we will all give up. If I win, you'll become our prisoners."

When they heard this, all the Hebrew soldiers were

"You have a sword and spear," David answered. "But I have God to protect me."

Then David took his slingshot and shot a stone at Goliath. It hit him on his forehead, and he fell over and died.

"I won!" shouted David. Then he cut off Goliath's head.

afraid. Only David was brave enough to say, "I'm not afraid. I'll go out and fight him."

For his weapon, David took his slingshot and a few stones.

Goliath made fun of David when he saw him and said, "Do you think that I'm only a dog, to come against me with a stick?"

King David

David became a great soldier and he saved the people from the Philistines many times. But King Saul grew jealous of David, and tried to kill him with a spear.

David was surprised and ran away. He had to stay in hiding for several years, be-cause Saul was looking for him. Once David found King Saul sleeping in a tent, and he saw a spear near him. To show his respect for the king, David didn't hurt Saul. But he took the spear and a water jug to show that he had been there. When Saul woke up, he realized what had happened and asked David to forgive him.

Then war broke out again. Saul got worried. He asked God for help, but got no answer. Then he decided to go see a woman who was a witch.

"How can I help you?" she asked him.

"Bring Samuel here!" answered Saul.

Samuel had been dead a long time, but the witch brought him back. "Saul, why have you called me?" Samuel asked.

"I'm very, very afraid," Saul said. "The Philistines are going to attack us, and God is no longer helping me."

"That's because you disobeyed God," Samuel told him. "Tomorrow you will lose the battle."

King Solomon

Saul died in the battle that day. David became the king. His palace was in the city of Jerusalem. Many years later, David died, and his son Solomon became king.

One day, God appeared to Solomon in a dream and said to him, "Ask for whatever you want, and I will give it to you."

"My God," replied Solomon, "you have chosen me to be king like my father David. But I am young and have no experience. I need help to lead this great people. Help me to know what is good and what is bad, so that I can lead them well."

God was pleased with what Solomon asked and said, "Because you have asked me for this, I will give you a very wise heart. Not only that, I will make you rich and important, so that no other king will be like you. If you obey my commands and follow my advice, you will be king for a long time."

With the help of God, Solomon was a very wise leader. He chose good people to give him advice. After four years Solomon began to build a temple in Jerusalem.

"I am pleased that you want to build the temple for me," God told him. "If you keep listening to me, I promise that I will always stay with my people."

After the temple was built, Solomon put the Ark of the Covenant in it.

Then he held a great celebration with everyone who had worked on the temple. He also offered gifts to God.

The Wisdom of Solomon

One day, two women came to the palace. One of them carried a dead baby in her arms. The other one held a healthy, living baby. Solomon asked them what they wanted. One of them said, "I live in the same house with her, and I had a baby boy. Three days later, she also had a son. This living baby is mine. Hers died during the night. But when I was sleeping, she switched the babies. She gave me the dead one, and took the living one for herself."

"That's not true!" the other woman screamed. "You're a liar!"

Solomon thought for a while. Then he said to one of his guards, "Go get a sword and cut the living baby in two. Give half to one woman, and half to the other."

"Oh, no, my king!" shouted the real mother. "Don't kill him!"

"Yes, divide him in two," said the other woman.

Then the king said, "Give the baby to the first woman, because she is the real mother." Solomon had tricked them so that he could tell who the real mother was.

The Queen of Sheba

Everybody at the palace admired King Solomon for making such good decisions. Even the Queen of a far-away country called Sheba heard about Solomon. She wanted to know more about him and decided to go to Jerusalem. She went with many servants and camels.

After she had stayed at Solomon's palace a while, she said, "I can see that everything people say about you is true. How wonderful God is, who has chosen you."

Then the queen gave King Solomon some gifts—one hundred twenty pieces of gold, besides jewels and a lot of spices. King Solomon gave her many gifts too.

With all the gold, Solomon made two hundred golden shields. He also had a throne of ivory made.

Seeing all this, the people said, "We've never seen such a beautiful palace as this."

Because of his wisdom and

money, Solomon was a power-
ful king. But he brought many
women into the palace who
prayed to false gods. God was
not pleased and told Solomon,
"You must not bring in these
women, because you will begin to pray to their gods."

The Punishment of Solomon

Solomon didn't pay attention to God's warnings. Instead, he did what he wanted to. To please the women, he built places for them to pray to their false gods. And he prayed to those gods, too. God was displeased at this and told him, "Because you have disobeyed me, after you die I will give your kingdom to your servant. But because of my love for your father David, I won't take away the whole kingdom."

As long as Solomon was alive, the country stayed together. When he died, his

son Rehoboam became king. Rehoboam treated the people badly, so they became angry at him.

A man named Jeroboam had worked for Solomon. He had been in charge of building a strong city wall for the king. Now Jeroboam made himself the leader of the people who didn't like Solomon's son. He became king of most of the Hebrew people. Rehoboam was king over the two tribes of Benjamin and Judah.

Jeroboam also disobeyed God, and so did the other kings who followed him. One of them was Ahab. He and his wife Jezebel tried to have the prophet Elijah killed. The prophet had to run away. He hid by a stream near the Jordan River. "Don't be afraid of anything," God told Elijah. "You can drink from the stream, and I'll send ravens to bring you food."

Then, to punish Ahab, God kept rain from falling on the country. Everything dried up.

The Prophet Elijah

No rain came for three years. At the end of this time, God sent the prophet Elijah to the king. When Ahab saw Elijah, he asked him, "Are you the one who has brought this trouble to Israel?"

"No!" Elijah replied. "It's because you and your family have forgotten the command-ments of God."

"Don't you know that I can punish you for saying this?" the king asked angrily.

"I know that you can pun-ish me," said Elijah. "But you can't bring back the rain."

"Then what should I do?" asked Ahab.

"Get all the people together

84

on Mount Carmel," Elijah told him.

When everyone was there, Elijah said, "Pray to your false gods to send fire down from heaven to burn this wood. Instead, I'll call on the real God—the God of Israel."

The prophets of the false gods began to pray. But nothing happened.

"Shout louder!" Elijah teased them. "Perhaps your god is asleep or away on a journey." They shouted louder, but still nothing happened.

Then Elijah prayed to the God of Israel. Suddenly, a great fire came down from the sky and set the wood on fire.

"The Lord is the true God!" all the people cried out.

Just then, clouds filled the sky and rain poured down. The people could grow food again.

The Chariot of Fire

Ahab was amazed. He told his wife Jezebel about everything that had happened. Jezebel was angry. She said she would kill Elijah. The prophet had to run away into the desert. After walking for a long time, Elijah was tired. He felt very hungry and thirsty. He was worn out and asked God to let him die.

Suddenly an angel appeared, holding a loaf of bread and a jug of water. "Get up and eat," the angel said. "You still have a long way to go."

Elijah felt better after eating and drinking. He went on his way again. When he got to Mount Sinai, he was surprised to see an earthquake and feel strong winds. Then he heard a tiny whispering sound, and God told him, "I want you to take Elisha as your friend. He will be a prophet to take your place."

Elijah obeyed. Later, he

was walking with Elisha by the Jordan River. Horses and a burning cart came down from the sky and took Elijah to heaven. Elisha cried when he saw that his friend was gone. Then he picked up the coat that Elijah had dropped. He hit the water of the Jordan River with it and said, "Where is the Lord, the God of Elijah?"

It was a kind of prayer, and God answered it. The water divided and Elisha walked through the river on the stones.

The Patience of Job

Long ago, a man named Job lived in the country of Uz. He was a good man who never did anything bad. There is a story that one day, God said to one of his servants, "There's no one on earth as good as Job!"

"I don't think so," the servant answered. "If you take away all his money, he won't love you anymore."

God then said to his servant, "I will let you destroy his sheep and goats and the other things he owns."

The servant destroyed Job's animals and wealth. Then he caused a great wind to spring up from the desert. It was so strong that it knocked down the house where Job's sons and daughters were having a party. They all

died. After all this, Job became sick and very sad. But he did not complain against God.

But Job's wife began to complain. "Why do you keep on praising God?" she asked angrily.

"Why not?" Job said. "We accept good things from God, so why shouldn't we also accept the bad?"

God was pleased by this. He rewarded Job for staying his friend. Job got better. He became rich again, and started a new family.

The Three Young Men in the Furnace

One time, the Hebrew people were sent to another country, called Babylonia. Nebuchadnezzar was the king of Babylonia.

He didn't worship the real God. The king had a statue of gold built and told his people, "You must pray to this idol. When you hear the sound of the trumpets, kneel down and pray. Anyone who does not obey will be thrown into a white-hot furnace to be burned alive."

"Then we will be burned alive!" said three young Hebrew men. They refused to pray to the false god. In anger, the king had them thrown into the furnace.

But to everyone's surprise, they walked around in the flames praising God. The king then said, "Come out of the flames! How wonderful is your God, who can save you from fire. From now on, anyone who speaks badly about your God will be punished."

Some time after this, Nebuchadnezzar had a dream about a tall tree that was cut down. It disturbed him and he asked the magicians in his palace to explain it, but they couldn't. Finally a young Hebrew named Daniel told the king what the dream meant.

"The tree which you saw in the dream is you, your majesty. You will lose your money and power for seven years, so you will understand that the real king of the world is God. You must make up for your sins by good deeds and by being kind to the poor."

91

Daniel in the Lions' Den

Later, there was another king named Darius in the land of Babylonia. Darius liked Daniel and made him an important person in his country. But other people became jealous of Daniel. They said that Daniel was an enemy because he would not pray to their false gods. Darius did not want to punish Daniel, but the law said he had to. So he ordered that Daniel be thrown into a den of lions. Once Daniel was inside, the king's soldiers blocked the entrance with a big stone.

The king felt very sad and couldn't eat or sleep. All night he thought about Daniel and the lions. The next morning when he woke up, Darius hurried to the den to find out what had happened. To his great surprise, he saw Daniel still alive and unhurt.

Darius was happy and ordered that Daniel be freed. He asked him, "Why didn't you get hurt?"

"I haven't done anything bad, either against God or against you, my king," Daniel said. "So God sent an angel to close the lions' mouths so they couldn't harm me."

Darius was glad. He punished the people who had said Daniel was bad.

Jonah and the Whale

This is a story about a Hebrew prophet. His name was Jonah. God told Jonah, "Go to the great city of Nineveh, and tell the people that I am unhappy about the bad things they are doing."

But Jonah didn't want to go there. He ran away and got on a boat going in the other direction. God caused a big storm with strong winds to spring up. The sailors were afraid that the ship would go down. They threw their cargo overboard. They knew that God had sent the storm, since Jonah had told them he was running away from God. So they asked Jonah, "What should we do with you, so that the storm will end?"

"Throw me into the sea," he answered, "and it will quiet down."

"We don't want to die be-

94

cause of this," they said. But they threw Jonah into the sea. A big fish swam by and swallowed Jonah. Jonah stayed in the fish for three days and three nights.

Jonah was sorry for what he had done and asked God to help him. So the Lord made the fish spit Jonah up on the shore. Then Jonah went to Nineveh and told the people, "Be sorry for your sins, or else God will destroy your city!"

The people listened to Jonah and tried to show that they were sorry. God saw this and did not punish them.

Zechariah and Elizabeth

Many years later, the Romans conquered the Hebrews' land. The Hebrews had to pay money to the Romans. They could not get free. So they hoped that someone would come and save them. They wanted a Savior.

An old priest named Zechariah lived at this time. An angel came from God and told Zechariah, "Your wife

Elizabeth is going to have a son. You'll name him John."

Zechariah was surprised and asked, "How is that possible? My wife and I are too old to have children!"

"With God, nothing is impossible," the angel told him. "But because you have doubted, you will not be able to speak until the child is born."

Just as the angel had said,

Zechariah and Elizabeth had a son. He was sent by God. Soon after the baby was born, another miracle happened. Zechariah could speak again.

The baby would grow up to become John the Baptist. God had chosen John to prepare the way for the Savior. John would baptize people in the Jordan River. He would also tell people to be sorry for their sins.

The Four Evangelists

This is the end of the first part of the Bible. It is called the Old Testament. The rest of the stories in this book are taken from the New Testament. Four writers called *evangelists* wrote about what Jesus said and did.

The names of the evangelists were Matthew, Mark, Luke and John. You can find the evangelists in this picture. There is an angel with Matthew, a lion with Mark, an ox (like a cow) with Luke and an eagle with John.

Part Two
The New Testament

The Announcement to Mary

The story of Jesus began around two thousand years ago. At that time, a girl named Mary lived in the town of Nazareth. She was engaged to a carpenter named Joseph. They were planning to get married soon.

One day, the angel Gabriel came to see Mary. He said,

"I've come to tell you great news, Mary. You are going to have a son and you'll name him Jesus."

"How can that be?" Mary asked. "I have no husband."

"The Holy Spirit will come down upon you," the angel answered. "So your son will be the Son of God."

On the Way to Bethlehem

Soon, Mary went to visit her cousin Elizabeth. Elizabeth was happy to see Mary and said, "You are blessed among all women, Mary. Blessed is the child in your womb." Elizabeth meant that God had done something special for Mary. Mary's baby would be very dear to God.

When Mary got back to Nazareth, Joseph realized that she was going to have a baby. This made him sad. Joseph

was not the father of the baby. He decided to quietly break their engagement. But an angel told him in a dream, "Don't be afraid to take Mary into your house. The Holy Spirit has given her this child. You must call the boy Jesus, because he will save his people from their sins." (Jesus means "God saves.")

Soon the king of Rome, who was called the emperor, made a law which said, "Everybody must go back to the town where his or her family came from. We want to count all the people." Joseph obeyed this command and got ready to make the trip.

He had Mary ride on a donkey, and they traveled to Bethlehem. That was the home town of Joseph's family. When they got there, Joseph saw how tired Mary was. He tried to find a place for her to rest. But many people had crowded into town and filled all the hotel rooms.

The Birth
of Jesus

Mary knew that it was almost
time for the baby to be born.
Joseph knocked at the door of
the last hotel. "Please give us
a place to stay, just for the
night," he asked.

"Sorry, all the rooms are
taken," the owner told them.
"Don't you have even a
small corner somewhere?"
Joseph insisted.
"Look around and you'll

104

see there's no space for you," answered the owner.

They finally found a stable with a donkey and some cattle. Mary's son was born there that night.

Mary wrapped Jesus in pieces of cloth and put him in a manger. It was cold, but the animals kept Jesus warm with their breath.

A bright star shone in the sky and the angels sang. That night was special, different from all other nights. On that night, the first Christmas, Jesus our Savior was born.

and an angel appeared. The shepherds were afraid. But the angel told them, "Don't be afraid, because I'm bringing you good news of great joy. Today a baby has been born, whose name is Jesus. He will be your Savior."

The shepherds heard angels singing in the night, "Glory to God in the highest, and peace on earth to people of good will."

Then the angels left and

The Shepherds

Not far from the stable, shepherds were watching their sheep. Some of them were resting, and others sat around the fire talking. Suddenly, a great light shone in the sky

106

everything was quiet. The
shepherds asked each other,
"What should we do?"

"Let's go to Bethlehem to
see this wonderful event,"
suggested some of them.

So the shepherds went to
the stable. There they found
Mary and Joseph and the
child. Jesus was lying in a
manger. They offered him gifts
and gave thanks to God. "At
last, the Savior has come!"
they said.

The Three Kings

The king of the Hebrews was Herod. One day, he received a visit from three kings from the East. They asked Herod, "Where is the newborn king of the Hebrews?"

"I don't know," said King Herod. Then he asked the smartest people he knew. They said that the king would be born in Bethlehem.

Herod asked the three kings, "How did you get here, since you came so far?"

"A star led us here," they told him.

Then Herod said, "If it's true that the Savior has been born, find him. When you have found him, come back here right away and let me know. I'll go to honor him too."

The three kings—whom we call Gaspar, Melchior and Balthazar—promised to tell Herod the news when they found the Savior.

They arrived at Bethlehem. Full of joy, they saw Mary and her son Jesus. They knelt down and offered him gifts of gold, frankincense and myrrh. Those were precious gifts to the people of that time. Then an angel warned them that Herod was jealous of the baby and wanted to kill him. So they went back to the East by another route.

The Flight into Egypt

When Herod didn't hear from the three kings, he became angry. He decided to look for the baby himself. An angel appeared in a dream and warned Joseph, "Get up, take the child and Mary, and hurry to Egypt. Herod is looking for the child to kill him." Joseph obeyed and left for Egypt, with Mary and Jesus.

Herod ordered his soldiers to kill all the baby boys in Bethlehem who would have been born around the same time as Jesus. So all those babies were killed. They hadn't done anything wrong, but Herod was very cruel.

For several years Mary,

Joseph and Jesus lived in Egypt. Finally, an angel appeared again in a dream and told Joseph, "Herod is dead. Now you don't have to be afraid of him anymore. Take the child and Mary, and go back to the land of Israel."

Obediently, they returned to Nazareth. Jesus grew up. He was close to his Father, God. He worked with Joseph as a carpenter. Protected by God, the little family lived happily together. Their home was full of peace and love. Jesus lived in Nazareth, so he was called a Nazarene.

Jesus in the Temple

Each year during the special celebration called the Passover, Mary and Joseph would go to Jerusalem to pray in the temple. They thanked God for everything he did for his people at the time of Moses. When Jesus was twelve, he went to Jerusalem with them.

As soon as the celebration was over, Mary and Joseph started back to Jerusalem with their relatives and friends. But on the way, they realized that Jesus was missing. They were worried and started to look for him among the other travelers. Then they

went back to Jerusalem. By now, they were very anxious.

They finally found Jesus in the temple. He was with the teachers, listening to them and asking them questions. "How can a boy of his age speak so wisely?" the teachers wondered.

"My son," Mary cried out when she saw him, "At last we've found you! We've looked everywhere for you."

"Why did you look for me?" Jesus asked. "Didn't you know that I must do what concerns my Father?"

Then he went back to Nazareth with Mary and Joseph. He continued to grow. God and all the people saw that he was very wise.

The Baptism of Jesus

When Jesus had grown up, John the Baptist, the son of Zechariah and Elizabeth, began his work. John went through the country by the Jordan River, talking to crowds of people.

They came to listen to him speak about the Savior who was coming. "You must always obey God's commandments and be sorry for your sins," John said.

"Who are you?" people asked him. "Are you the Savior?"

"No," John answered. "I baptize with water, but the

Savior will baptize with the Holy Spirit."

When Jesus was about thirty years old, he went to the river and asked John to baptize him.

"Why have you come to me? I should be baptized by you," John said.

"No," Jesus told him. "We must do everything that God asks."

Jesus stepped into the river, and John baptized him. Just then, a light shone in the sky. John saw a dove over Jesus' head. A voice from the sky said, "This is my son, whom I love. I am very pleased with him."

Jesus came out of the water, and the Holy Spirit told him to go into the desert.

The Temptation of Jesus

In the desert, Jesus prayed for forty days. He did not eat. Then the devil tried to make Jesus do something that God didn't want. The devil told Jesus, "You can eat if you want to. Do you see these stones? If you are the Son of God, change them into bread."

But Jesus answered, "People don't live only on bread, but on the Word of God."

Then the devil took Jesus to the top of the temple in Jerusalem and said, "If you are the Son of God, throw yourself down from here.

The angels will come and save you."

But Jesus answered, "God's word says, 'You shall not try to test the Lord your God.'"

Finally, the devil took Jesus to the top of a high mountain and showed him all the nations of the world. The devil said, "I'll give you all these countries if you kneel down and pray to me."

Jesus told him, "Get away from me! God's Word says to pray to *him*!"

The devil left. Angels came and brought Jesus something to eat. Then Jesus left the desert.

117

The Big Catch of Fish

Jesus went around like John and talked to crowds of people. He said, "Be sorry for your sins. God is near in a special way." One day while Jesus was walking along the shore of the Sea of Galilee, he saw two fishermen. They were Simon and his brother Andrew. "Come and follow me," Jesus told them, "and I will make you fishermen for people." A little later, Jesus saw two other brothers, James and John. "Come with me," he told them.

Another time, Jesus was talking to the people near the Lake of Gennesaret. He saw Peter's boat. Jesus climbed into the boat. When they were out on the lake, Jesus said to them, "Throw your nets into the sea!"

"Teacher," said Peter, "we've been fishing all night long and haven't caught anything. But if you say so, we'll throw the nets in anyway."

So they put the nets into the water. They caught so many fish that the nets began to break. "Come and help us!" Peter cried out to James and John in their boat.

Then Peter knelt down in front of Jesus. "Leave me, Lord. I'm not good enough for you."

But Jesus told him, "Don't be afraid. From now on, you'll be catching people."

The Twelve Apostles

Jesus often went outside to pray. Sometimes he would spend the whole night praying. One morning after praying, Jesus chose twelve of his followers to be especially close to him. He called them "apostles." Jesus told Peter, "You used to be called Simon, but now you will be called Peter." The other apostles were Andrew, James, John, Philip, Bartholomew, Matthew, Thomas, another James, Simon the Zealot, Judas the son of James, and Judas Iscariot.

When Jesus came down from the mountain, he found a large crowd waiting for him. They wanted to hear Jesus

speak, and hoped he would cure the sick people. Jesus healed many of them. Everyone wanted to touch him, because he had the power to heal.

There was one day in the week, called the sabbath, when people weren't supposed to do any work. On one sabbath day, Jesus saw a sick man. The man's hand was hurt. Some people who were called Pharisees asked Jesus if it was all right to heal someone on the sabbath day. Jesus said it was all right to do good deeds on the sabbath. Then he turned to the sick man and said, "Hold out your hand." The man did so and he was healed. The Pharisees didn't like that.

Herod's Revenge

By this time there was another king named Herod. He was a son of the Herod who had ordered the killing of the babies in Bethlehem. The new king wasn't very good either. He had taken his brother's wife for himself. John the Baptist had told him, "It's not right for you to marry her."

So King Herod had thrown John into prison. Herod's wife said, "You should kill John!"

"No, I don't dare do that," Herod answered. "The people would be angry."

On Herod's birthday they had a big party. Many people were there. Herod's step-daughter Salome did a dance which Herod enjoyed. He liked it so much that he told her, "Ask for anything you want, and I'll give it to you."

Salome asked her mother what to say. Then she told Herod, "Give me the head of John the Baptist."

The king didn't want to do this and was sorry he had made the promise. But because he had promised in front of all those people, Herod ordered that John be killed.

John's friends went and told Jesus the sad news.

The Wedding at Cana

One time, Jesus and Mary were invited to a wedding in the town of Cana. At one point, Mary noticed that they had run out of wine. So she went to Jesus and said, "They have no more wine."

Jesus answered, "What is that to me and to you? My time isn't here yet."

But Mary turned to the servants and said, "Do whatever he tells you."

Jesus told them, "Fill those jars with water." He pointed to six large stone jars. The servants filled them. "Now take some out," said Jesus.

"Bring it to the headwaiter." The water had been changed into wine!

The headwaiter tasted the wine and was surprised at how good it was. But he didn't know where it had come from. He went to the bridegroom and told him, "People usually serve the best wine first. But you have kept the best wine for last."

The Miracle of the Bread

More and more people came to listen to Jesus. Once a large crowd had followed him. But they had nothing to eat for three days. "Teacher," one of the apostles said to Jesus, "where are we going to get enough bread to feed all of these people?"

"There's nothing here but five loaves and two fish," Andrew added.

"Bring them to me," Jesus told them.

In front of the crowd, Jesus blessed the bread and the fish. He gave them to the people to eat. Everybody had enough! Jesus had done a miracle and multiplied the bread.

Jesus also worked many other miracles. A miracle is a wonderful action that only God can do. Jesus brought a young girl back to life, healed sick people who touched him, and gave sight to blind people. Everyone was surprised to see deaf people hear, lame people walk and blind people begin to see again.

Jesus also felt sorry for simple people who lived hard lives. He told them, "Come to me, everybody who works hard and has a lot of troubles. I will give you rest. Learn from me, for I am gentle and humble of heart, and you will find peace."

Jesus Walks on the Water

After this Jesus went up a mountain to pray. The apostles went out to sea in their boat. It was night. Before they could get to shore, a storm came. "The waves are rocking the boat!" Peter cried out.

Jesus was on the shore and saw the apostles' boat bobbing up and down in the waves. He came walking toward them on the water.

"Who is that coming?" they wondered.

"It's a ghost!" they screamed.

But Jesus came closer and said, "Don't be afraid! It's me."

"Lord," Peter shouted, "if it's really you, let me come to you on the water."

"All right," Jesus answered, "come!"

So Peter got out of the boat and started walking on the

water toward Jesus. But soon he began to realize how strong the wind was, and how high the waves were. He became afraid and began to sink. "Save me, Lord!" he shouted.

Right away, Jesus put out his hand and caught Peter. Jesus asked him, "Why did

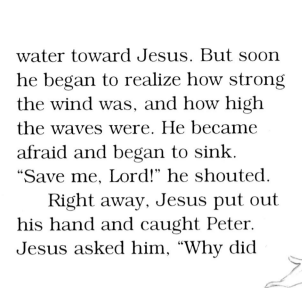

you doubt? You don't have much faith at all."

Then they walked back to the boat and got in. The wind began to calm down, and the apostles said, "He is really the Son of God."

The Transfiguration of Jesus

Jesus told his apostles, "If you want to help other people, follow me. Don't be proud. Then you will want to come with me."

One day Jesus took Peter, James and John with him to the top of a high mountain. Jesus became different. His face lit up like the sun, and his clothes became as white as snow. Moses and the prophet Elijah also appeared, standing on each side of Jesus.

"Lord!" Peter cried out, "it's good that we are here. If you want, I'll set up three tents—one for you, one for Moses and one for Elijah."

Just then, a low cloud came right over them and they heard a voice which said, "This is my Son whom I love. Listen to him."

The three apostles shook with fear when they heard this and hid their faces. "Get up and don't be afraid," Jesus told them. "But don't tell any-body about what you have seen, until the day when I rise from the dead."

Then they went back down the mountain. Jesus told them, "I will be turned over to people who will hurt me and kill me. But on the third day I will rise from the dead." When they heard this, the apostles felt sad.

The Parables of Jesus

Jesus often talked to the people about how to live. To help them understand better, he told stories which we call *parables.* One of them is the story of the Good Samaritan.

On the way to Jericho, a Hebrew man was attacked by robbers who beat him up and left him to die. A priest came down the road and saw the man, but didn't stop to help him. Neither did a priest's helper, who also passed by. But one of the Samaritans stopped to help. The Samaritans were enemies of the Hebrews. The Samaritan poured oil into the Hebrew man's wounds to help them heal and

brought him to a hotel to get better.

Jesus asked the crowd, "Of the three, who was a neighbor to the man who was hurt?"

"The one who helped him," someone answered.

"Then go and do the same," Jesus said.

Jesus told another parable about the Prodigal Son. This son asked for part of his father's money, then went away and wasted it. When he became poor and came back home, his father held a big party to celebrate his son's return. But the older son, who had never left home, felt jealous and grew angry. "This isn't fair," he complained to his father. "I've always stayed home to help you, and you never gave me a big party like this."

"But everything I have is yours," the father said. "Your brother was lost and has been found. So I had to celebrate and be happy!"

133

Jesus Welcomes Children

Jesus used to walk through the country with the apostles. One time, he heard them arguing about which of them was the most important.

Jesus told them that whoever wants to be first with people will be the last with God. Then Jesus saw some children and said, "Anyone who receives a little child like this for my sake receives me; and whoever receives me, receives my Father who sent me."

Another time Jesus saw that the apostles were sending some children away. Jesus

134

stopped the apostles and told them, "Let the little children come to me, for the kingdom of heaven belongs to them."

Another time Jesus asked the apostles, "Who do people say that I am?"

They answered, "Some say John the Baptist, and others say the prophet Elijah."

"But you," he asked them, "who do you say that I am?"

"You are the Savior, the real Son of God," Peter declared.

"God has been good to you, Peter," Jesus answered. "My Father in heaven has helped you to know this. And I tell you that you are rock, and on this rock I will build my Church. The power of the devil will not be able to destroy it." Then Jesus added, "I will give you the keys of the kingdom of heaven."

The Raising of Lazarus

Jesus had some friends named Martha, Mary and Lazarus. They were two sisters and a brother. One day Jesus got a message that Lazarus was very sick.

Jesus said, "His sickness will not end in death. It is for the glory of God." When Jesus got to their house, Martha came out to meet him. She felt sad because Lazarus had died. She told Jesus, "Lord, if you had been here, Lazarus wouldn't have died. But even now, I know that God will give you whatever you ask."

"Lazarus will rise again," Jesus said.

"Yes," Martha said, "I know that he'll rise again on the last day."

Mary came out to see Jesus. She was crying. Jesus began to cry too. Then Jesus went to the tomb with them. He told some men, "Take away the stone." The men rolled away the big stone

that closed the tomb.

Then Jesus prayed to his Father in heaven and shouted, "Lazarus, come out!"

Lazarus walked out of the tomb! Everyone was amazed.

Later, Jesus went to visit them again. Mary took some perfume and washed Jesus' feet with it.

When the apostle named Judas saw this, he complained, "What a waste! That perfume could have been sold and the money given to the poor."

But Jesus told him, "There will always be poor people around, but I won't always be here with you."

Jesus Enters Jerusalem

It was time for the Passover celebration. Jesus sent two of his followers into a nearby village to get a donkey that was tied up there.

"What if someone asks us why we're taking it?" they asked.

"Tell them that the Lord needs it," Jesus answered.

So the disciples got the donkey and came back with it. They put a cloth on it and Jesus began to ride into Jerusalem. When the crowd saw him coming, they shouted with joy. They waved palm branches in the air and cried out, "Blessed is he who comes in the name of the Lord!"

This happened to make something come true which the prophets had said a long time before, "Your king will come to you riding on a donkey."

All of this made the Pharisees angry. They complained to Jesus, "Tell the people to be quiet."

But Jesus told them, "If they were silent, even the stones would cry out."

So while Jesus entered Jerusalem with the happy crowd, the Pharisees made plans to have Jesus killed.

Jesus Sends the Business People out of the Temple

Jesus went into the temple in Jerusalem. He saw people selling cows, sheep and doves. What a noise there was! Jesus grew angry and chased those people out of the temple. When somebody asked why Jesus was doing this, he said, "The temple is a house for prayer, but you have turned it into a place for making money!"

Some people saw this and tried to think how to get rid of Jesus. But right then they couldn't do anything. The crowds of people liked Jesus.

When Jesus came back to the temple again, the priests

140

asked him a question. "Who said you could do these things?"

Jesus asked them a question they couldn't answer. Then he told them, "Neither will I tell you who said I could do these things."

The Last Supper

Jesus' enemies were still planning to kill him. They said, "We must get rid of him."

Jesus called two of the apostles and said, "Go and prepare a room where we can celebrate the Passover together." Right away the two of them went to set the table and get everything ready for the Passover meal.

That night Jesus sat at the table with the twelve apostles. This would be his last supper with them. He took a basin of water and a cloth, and washed

the apostles' feet.

During the meal, Jesus grew sad and said, "One of you will hurt me."

"Am I the one, Teacher?" each of them asked.

Peter asked John to find out who it was, and Jesus said, "It's the one to whom I will hand a little piece of bread." And he gave the bread to Judas.

"Am I the one, Teacher?" Judas asked.

"You said it," Jesus answered. Then he added, "Do quickly what you are going to do."

Then Judas left the room while the others watched him.

The Holy Eucharist

During the meal, Jesus took bread, blessed it, broke it and gave it to the apostles. He said, "Take and eat; this is my body."

Then he took a cup of wine and blessed it, and gave it to them saying, "Take and drink; this is my blood." With these words, Jesus gave us the Holy Eucharist. When we receive Communion, we receive Jesus' body and blood, even though it looks and tastes like bread and wine.

Meanwhile, Judas had gone to some important people and told them where they

144

could find Jesus. They paid Judas thirty silver coins.

After the meal, Jesus and the apostles went to the Garden of Gethsemane to pray. On the way, he told them, "Tonight your faith in me will be shaken, just like sheep are scattered when the shepherd is hurt. But I will rise again, and will meet you in Galilee."

"Everyone else may leave you, Lord, but I never will," Peter declared.

"Peter," Jesus told him, "before the roosters crow tomorrow morning, you will say three times that you don't know me."

"No I won't!" said Peter. "Even if I have to die with you, I'll never do that." And all the others said the same thing.

The Agony in the Garden

When they got to the Garden of Gethsemane, Jesus told the apostles, "Stay here and keep awake. I'm going over there to pray."

Jesus went off by himself. He felt sad and even afraid. He prayed, "Father, take away the suffering that is coming. But

do what *you* want, not what I want."

Then Jesus went back to the apostles. He found them sleeping. So he woke them up and asked them to pray. Two more times, Jesus went back to pray. He began to shake and to sweat drops of blood.

Then he heard soldiers coming. Jesus told the apostles, "Now my time has come." They saw Judas with the soldiers. Judas had told the soldiers, "Arrest the man I will kiss."

Judas went up to Jesus and kissed him on the cheek.

The soldiers rushed up and took hold of Jesus. Then Peter took out his sword and hurt a man standing nearby.

"Put away your sword," Jesus told Peter. "Anybody who uses a sword will die by a sword." Then Jesus touched the man who was hurt and healed him. Jesus said to the soldiers, "You have come to get me as if I were a thief. But all the while I was teaching in the temple you never touched me."

They led Jesus away. The apostles were afraid and ran.

The Trial of Jesus

Jesus was brought to the Hebrew leaders. They asked Jesus questions. One of them asked, "Are you really the Savior, the Son of God?"

"Yes, I am," Jesus said.

"He has committed a sin!" said one of the leaders.

"He should be killed!" said someone else. Then these people made fun of Jesus and slapped him.

Meanwhile, Peter was nearby but tried not to let people notice him. A servant girl saw him and asked in front of several people, "Aren't you one of this man's followers?"

"No, you've made a mis-take," Peter said. "I don't know him."

People asked him two more times. Each time, Peter said that he didn't know Jesus. "I don't know what you're talking about," he said, "I don't know him!"

After the third time, Peter heard a rooster crow. Then he remembered what Jesus had said, "You will say three times that you don't know me." Peter felt very sorry. He went out and cried because of what he had done.

Pilate, the Roman Governor

The soldiers brought Jesus to Pontius Pilate, the Roman governor. Pilate asked Jesus questions. Pilate could see that Jesus was good. He wanted to let Jesus go. The Romans usually set some prisoner free for the feast of Passover. A man named

Barabbas was in jail. Barabbas had killed somebody and caused a lot of trouble. Pilate asked the people, "Who do you want me to free— Barabbas or Jesus?"

"Free Barabbas!" they cried out. "Crucify Jesus!" ("Crucify" means to kill on a cross.)

Pilate ordered the soldiers to take Jesus away and hit him with straps. The soldiers also pushed a crown of sharp thorns down onto Jesus' head. They made fun of Jesus. "Hello, king!" they said.

After Jesus had been hurt with the straps and thorns, Pilate had him brought back to the crowd. He hoped the crowd would feel sorry for Jesus. But the crowd shouted again, "Crucify him!"

"Do you want me to crucify your king?" Pilate demanded.

"Our only king is the emperor!" they shouted.

Pilate's wife asked him to leave Jesus alone. But Pilate was afraid that the emperor would take away his job. He told the soldiers to crucify Jesus. But he washed his hands to show that he didn't want to take the blame for this.

The Way to Calvary

Jesus began to walk toward the hill called Calvary. He had to carry the cross on which he would die. People made fun of him and said mean things. But Jesus' friends cried.

Jesus met some women crying for him. He said to them, "Don't cry for me. Cry

for yourselves and for your children."

Sometimes Jesus fell because the cross was heavy. The soldiers kicked him to make him get up. But they were afraid that Jesus might die on the way. So they grabbed a man named Simon and made him help Jesus carry the cross.

Jesus had suffered very much. He had hardly any strength when he got to Calvary.

The Crucifixion

The soldiers nailed Jesus' hands and feet to the cross. Two thieves were crucified on either side of him. When Jesus' enemies saw him hanging on the cross, they made fun of him and said, "If you are really the Son of God, come down from there and save yourself." One of the thieves also said mean things. But the other one said, "Jesus, remember me when you will be king."

"This day you will be with me in heaven," Jesus told him.

His mother Mary stood by the cross, along with Mary Magdalene and some other women. Jesus saw John the apostle standing there too and he said to Mary, "There is your son." Turning to John, Jesus added, "There is your mother."

The crowd kept making fun of Jesus. They laughed at him. "So you're the Savior!" they shouted. "Come down from the cross and then we'll believe in you."

Jesus Dies on the Cross

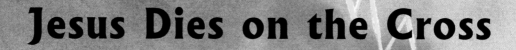

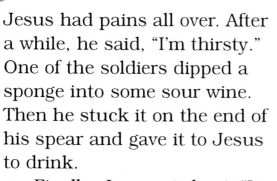

Jesus had pains all over. After a while, he said, "I'm thirsty." One of the soldiers dipped a sponge into some sour wine. Then he stuck it on the end of his spear and gave it to Jesus to drink.

Finally, Jesus cried out, "It is finished! Father, I put my life into your hands." Then he died.

Everything got dark. There was an earthquake and a cracking sound. The soldiers were afraid and said, "He really was the Son of God!"

One of them then stuck his spear into Jesus' side, to make sure he was dead. Then a good man named Joseph of Arimathea took the body of Jesus down from the cross. He wrapped it in cloths. Then he brought it to a new tomb which had been cut out of rock. He and some other men put Jesus' body inside and rolled a big stone across the hole. Mary Magdalene and another woman watched. "We will come back," they said.

Jesus Rises from the Dead

The next day, Jesus' enemies went to see Pilate and said, "Before he died, Jesus told people that he would come back to life again in three days."

"Do you believe that?" Pilate asked them.

"No," they answered, "but tell the soldiers to watch the tomb for three days. That way, Jesus' friends can't come and steal his body, and then say that he rose."

Pilate agreed. So soldiers were sent to guard the tomb.

On the morning of the third day a great light shone. An angel came down from heaven and rolled the rock away from the entrance to the tomb. The tomb was empty. Jesus had risen from the dead!

Mary Magdalene and some other women came to the grave a short while later. They were so surprised when they saw the empty tomb! Then the angel came and said, "Don't be afraid! You are looking for Jesus, but he's not here. He is alive again."

The women were so happy! They ran to tell the good news to the apostles. On the way, they met Jesus. He told them, "Go and tell the apostles to go to Galilee to meet me."

Jesus Appears to the Apostles

The soldiers told Jesus' enemies about the empty tomb. Jesus' enemies paid the soldiers to keep quiet. "Don't tell anyone what happened," they ordered. "Say that Jesus' friends came during the night and stole his body."

Meanwhile, the apostles were together in a locked room. They were still afraid. Suddenly, they heard Jesus'

voice, "Peace be with you." There was Jesus!

"Is it really you, Lord?" they asked.

"Yes, it is," Jesus answered. "Just as the Father has sent me, I am sending you. Receive the Holy Spirit. If you forgive anyone's sins, they are forgiven." Jesus stayed with them for a little while. He even sat down and

ate something to show them he was alive. Then he disappeared.

Thomas had not been there. The others told him about Jesus' visit. But Thomas would not believe them. "I won't believe it unless I can see the nail marks in his hands and feet," Thomas said.

Jesus came back a few days later, and this time Thomas was there. Jesus told him, "Look at my hands and my feet and touch my side. Do you believe now?"

"My Lord and my God!" Thomas said. He got down on his knees.

Jesus Goes Back to Heaven

Jesus came to see the apostles a few times. He told them what he wanted them to do. He said, "You will soon receive the gift of the Holy Spirit. John baptized you with water. But soon you will be baptized with the Holy Spirit. You must go everywhere and tell the good news.

"Baptize people in the name of the Father, the Son and the Holy Spirit. Tell them everything that I have taught you. I will always be with you, even until the end of the world."

One day Jesus led his friends out to the Mount of Olives and blessed them. A great cloud appeared. Jesus rose into the air and disappeared into the clouds. The apostles kept looking at the sky. Suddenly two angels came and asked them, "Why are you looking into the sky? Jesus who has gone up into heaven will come back someday in the same way."

Then the apostles and Jesus' other friends went back to the big room where they had been staying. They chose a follower of Jesus named Matthias to take the place of Judas.

The Holy Spirit

The celebration called Pentecost came fifty days after Easter. The apostles had gathered for prayer in the upper room. Mary, the mother of Jesus, was with them. Suddenly, they heard a strong wind blowing right in the house. What looked like tongues of fire appeared over their heads. The Holy Spirit had come down upon them.

They ran out of the room and began to tell the good news of Jesus to the crowds of people in the streets. The Holy Spirit made them able to speak and understand different languages. Hearing this, the crowds wondered what had happened. People asked, "How can we all hear them in our own languages?" Many of them became followers of Jesus.

After that, the apostles traveled to far places telling people about Jesus. Peter went to Rome. Many people there became followers of Jesus. With the help of the Holy Spirit, Jesus' Church spread all over the world.

164

St. Paul Book & Media Centers

ALASKA
750 West 5th Ave., Anchorage, AK 99501   907-272-8183
CALIFORNIA
3908 Sepulveda Blvd., Culver City, CA 90230   310-397-8676
5945 Balboa Ave., San Diego, CA 92111   619-565-9181
46 Geary Street, San Francisco, CA 94108   415-781-5180
FLORIDA
145 S.W. 107th Ave., Miami, FL 33174   305-559-6715
HAWAII
1143 Bishop Street, Honolulu, HI 96813   808-521-2731
ILLINOIS
172 North Michigan Ave., Chicago, IL 60601   312-346-4228
LOUISIANA
4403 Veterans Memorial Blvd., Metairie, LA 70006   504-887-7631
MASSACHUSETTS
50 St. Paul's Ave., Jamaica Plain, Boston, MA 02130
617-522-8911
Rte. 1, 885 Providence Hwy., Dedham, MA 02026   617-326-5385
MISSOURI
9804 Watson Rd., St. Louis, MO 63126   314-965-3512
NEW JERSEY
561 U.S. Route 1, Wick Plaza, Edison, NJ 08817   908-572-1200
NEW YORK
150 East 52nd Street, New York, NY 10022   212-754-1110
78 Fort Place, Staten Island, NY 10301   718-447-5071
OHIO
2105 Ontario Street (at Prospect Ave.), Cleveland, OH 44115
610-621-9427
PENNSYLVANIA
510 Holstein Street, Bridgeport, PA 19405; 610-277-7728
SOUTH CAROLINA
243 King Street, Charleston, SC 29401   803-577-0175
TENNESSEE
4811 Poplar Ave., Memphis, TN 38117   901-761-2987
TEXAS
114 Main Plaza, San Antonio, TX 78205   210-224-8101
VIRGINIA
1025 King Street, Alexandria, VA 22314   703-549-3806
GUAM
285 Farenholt Avenue, Suite 308, Tamuning, Guam 96911;
671-649-4377
CANADA
3022 Dufferin Street, Toronto, Ontario, Canada M6B 3T5
416-781-9131